Defining
Sexism

IN THE U.S.

Elizabeth Hall Magill

Elizabeth Hall Magill
elizabeth.hallmagill@gmail.com
www.elizabethhallmagill.com

Book Layout ©2013 BookDesignTemplates.com
Cover Design by Longwood University Design Lab
Print Cover Design by Amelia McConnell
Author Photograph by Courtney Vogel Photography

Defining Sexism/ Elizabeth Hall Magill.—1st ed.
ISBN   978-1533079879

Contents

For Audrey, and for all our daughters

For Nicholas, and for all our sons

In our world, divide and conquer must become define and empower.

—AUDRE LORDE

DEFINING SEXISM

P eople who do the same work—plumbers, nurses, electricians, computer engineers—share an "insider's" understanding of that work. They use terms to describe important ideas, tools, and procedures. Those who don't share their work might not understand the terms, or might pick up a piece of information in conversation or in daily life without getting the whole picture. For example, the talk among a bunch of computer engineers about ways to solve the latest bugs in their software sounds like "shop talk" to the rest of us. The people who share this "shop talk" are part of a **discourse community**—a community of people who speak the same lingo about their work.

People who study sexism and work to eliminate it also share an "insider's" view of their work and use shared terms to discuss it. The common term to describe this discourse community is "feminist," but not all people who work to eliminate sexism name themselves feminists, for various reasons. In addition, their professions vary—they might be professors, journalists, authors, speakers, lawyers, or activists. Yet they all share a common understanding of what sexism is, how and where it functions in our culture, and how it affects each of us.

Unfortunately, our national discussions are often uncertain when it comes to sexism—is a particular joke sexist, or are the people (mostly women) who say it is just uptight? Is it sexist to think a political candidate who is about to become a grandmother might not run for president—but not to question the political goals of a grandfather? Are women really paid less than men for equal work, or do women simply gravitate toward lower-paying jobs?

We ask many questions about the consequences of sexism without realizing that they are connected to it at all. When we ask why boys are struggling with identity and performance in school, or why so many men feel frustrated and powerless even as they are told they have more power than women, we are wondering aloud about the consequences of sexism for boys and men—we just aren't connecting the dots between our questions and our answers.

We also often fail to connect the dots between sexism and other forms of discrimination, such as racism and homophobia. We make assumptions about sexism—for example, that all women experience it in the same way, or that men are naturally both sexist and violent—that limit our ability to address it effectively. Most of us aren't in on the shop talk among the people who study and speak about sexism and its consequences, so we don't even have the tools to connect those dots.

To discuss and address sexism in the United States, we must understand what it is and how it functions. We must all become insiders who can speak the lingo of those who study sexism. At its foundation, sexism is about power—not just individual power, but cultural and institutional power. Who shapes law and policy, and who is most deeply affected by that law and policy? Understanding that sexism and intersecting forms of discrimination are based in societal power structures is vital to understanding how discrimination works—and what we can do about it.

What is Sexism?

Sexism is the belief, institutionalized in laws and customs, that females are inferior to males. This belief supports and justifies the insult, shame, abuse, exclusion, dismissal, and unequal treatment of girls and women in every social, professional, and private space of a society. A society that is structured in this way—with laws and customs that give males more power and privileges—is called a **patriarchy**.

Sexism can be overt and subtle, conscious and unconscious, malicious and blind. Each time sexism is expressed—privately or publically, in support of a policy or an idea, or to degrade an individual female in a specific time and place—that expression reinforces the policies and practices that form the backbone of a patriarchy.

A patriarchy is not built on sexism alone, and sexism alone doesn't hold it together. Other forms of discrimination, such as racism and homophobia, are also built into the laws and customs of a patriarchy. Like sexism, these biases can be expressed consciously or unconsciously, and their expressions keep the patriarchy in place, allowing some people more freedoms and rights—more humanity—than others.

How is Sexism Connected to Power?

When most of us hear the word "power," we think of money and politics, influence and attention. We think of the boss, the CEO, the president. People who are movers and shakers, who have the ability to determine the course of history, or at least the course of lots of lives.

This is indeed one kind of power, and it is vital to keeping a patriarchy in place. But this type of sweeping power over others isn't the only power at play among human beings, and it isn't the only kind of power that allows sexism to thrive.

Types of Power

Because sexism is a belief built into laws and customs, it is intertwined with both kinds of human power: external and internal.

EXTERNAL POWER

For any individual, **external power** is power in the world—the ways in which we interact with others and make an impact on our communities. External power can affect the lives of a large number of people; for example, the power a judge has to uphold or change a law, or the power a CEO has to determine company policy. That's the sweeping power I described above. But external power can be less grand than that—in a relationship, this type of power can be as gentle as a loving parent making informed decisions for a child, or as cruel as a husband physically abusing his wife. Violence is often associated with this type of external power, as it is a force that can keep others from asserting power.

INTERNAL POWER

Internal power is the power that simply *belongs* to every person—the power that makes us human, with unique abilities and gifts. This power comes from within, and motivates us to act on our own behalf. Internal power stems from self-esteem, and is affected by our beliefs about ourselves. The external power that parents, teachers, and other adults have over children deeply influences their internal power, as it shapes their beliefs about themselves and their role in society. While it is possible (and often painful) to have internal power that does not translate to the external world, the point of personal empowerment is to create the conditions, both internal and external, that allow a person to flourish in a community. Without those conditions, internal power can be buried or forgotten.

That's why Alice Walker has said that the most common way people give up their power is by thinking they don't have any. Ms. Walker's insight speaks to the deep connection between internal and external power. If we hear (in movies, books, magazines, newspapers, advertisements, political speeches, video games, news shows, etc.) that we aren't good enough to do something, we might believe it. The resulting low self-esteem can become an inner barrier to even the most modest kind of external power. It's almost impossible to do something you think you can't do, and it takes a lot of internal struggle to believe you can do something, and then act on that belief, when you get external messages that you can't. In addition, if we are prevented from doing something that our internal power directs us to do—whether the "something" is a sport or a job or a major life decision—by those with political or financial power over others, we are blocked from gaining external power, sweeping or otherwise. (See "How Does Sexism Affect Self-Esteem?")

A sexist society—a patriarchy—relies on the manipulation of both kinds of power, so that those who are said to be inferior will not believe otherwise, and will not try to change the external conditions of their lives.

Power and Privilege

If you close your eyes and imagine a powerful person, chances are you think of a man. This man is probably white, good-looking, heterosexual, fit, and rich. He's somewhere between the ages of 25 and 70. The kind of man who, we imagine, can get things done just by walking into a room.

Does that mean that every straight white man in the U.S. feels endlessly powerful, able to act with ultimate authority, be with the woman of his dreams, and bring home the big bucks? Absolutely not—in fact, many men feel frustrated by pressure to live up to this image. (See "How is Sexism Vital to Traditional Masculinity?") But it does mean that anyone who has even one of the characteristics of this image (such as whiteness) has advantages in our culture. A person who can make assumptions related to having power—both externally and internally—within a patriarchy has **privilege**.

Just what does privilege look like? In her essay, "White Privilege and Male Privilege," Peggy McIntosh, Associate Director of the Wellesley College Center for Research on Women, lists 46 advantages she has as a white person in our culture. I've listed a few of her statements about her experience of white privilege below (taken at random from her list):[1]

- When I am told about our national heritage or about "civilization," I am shown that people of my color made it what it is.
- I did not have to educate our children to be aware of systemic racism for their own daily physical protection.
- I can swear, or dress in secondhand clothes, or not answer letters, without having people attribute these choices to the bad morals, the poverty, or the illiteracy of my race.
- I can worry about racism without being seen as self-interested or self-seeking.

- I can easily buy posters, postcards, picture books, greeting cards, dolls, toys, and children's magazines featuring people of my race.

McIntosh's list exposes the assumptions we make when we have privilege and the ways in which privilege can be invisible to those who have it.

DENYING PRIVILEGE

One of the surest signs of privilege is that you don't have to consider, and can actively deny, the existence of privilege. All those ways in which privilege can be invisible to those who hold it result from embodying a cultural norm of some kind—whiteness, maleness, heterosexuality, economic stability or affluence. Culturally, some characteristics (and the resulting perspectives) are assumed to be at the center of human experience. In her essay "Notes toward a Politics of Location," Adrienne Rich describes her experience with whiteness: "I was located by color and sex as surely as a Black child was located by color and sex—though the implications of white identity were mystified by the presumption that white people are the center of the universe."[2]

It is that idea—whiteness is the standard—that lies at the core of privilege. And it applies to all other elements of the standard as well—maleness, wealth, heterosexuality, body image, age, physical ability. As a person with one or more types of privilege—a white person, a heterosexual person, a male—it can be difficult to hear that you have privilege. The fact that you have privilege, or that you might harbor some unconscious bias toward others, can feel like an invitation to guilt or an accusation of conscious intolerance. The idea that you have an obligation to understand a system you benefit from but didn't invent, in addition to dealing with the difficulties the system creates for you, can be uncomfortable. But feeling uncomfortable, guilty, or defensive isn't what facing privilege is about—privilege is not an accusation at all. It is a fact of patriarchy, the flip side of what it feels like to be told you "throw like a girl" in a tone of disgust or viewed with suspicion and fear because of the color of your skin.

PRIVILEGE AND DEMOCRACY

All of this talk about privilege and patriarchy seems to fly in the face of who we say we are as a country. A system built on various forms of discrimination sounds downright un-American— aren't we a land of equal opportunity, where hard work will get you where you want to go? Aren't we—women as well as men— supposed to be what Michael Kimmel, author of *Manhood in America*, calls self-made men, people who have built solid lives on hard work and sacrifice?

Well, yes—that is how we conceive of ourselves as a nation. To say that a person has cultural advantages might seem to imply that our national self-image is wrong, and work isn't vital to success. For most people, privilege doesn't mean you didn't have to work hard to get where you are, or even that if you work hard you will definitely succeed. Building a business, finishing a degree, getting a job and growing professionally, owning and maintaining a home, putting kids through school—these are things that take dedication and responsibility on an individual level. But those with privilege—and as a white, middle-class, straight woman, I am aware that I have it on some levels even as I deal with sexism—can move through a world that assumes success equals hard work, and doesn't require you to push against cultural bias.

Many women begin to build their lives—attending school, working, having a child—only to come up against barriers of sexism, racism, and other forms of discrimination that can have serious physical and financial consequences.

- *Bene't Holmes:* Ms. Holmes is a single mother and a Walmart employee in Chicago. Her job includes lifting 50-pound boxes, which she was required to do even when pregnant, despite Walmart's written policies of pregnancy accommodation and Ms. Holmes' appeals to her employer that the work was unsafe for her pregnancy. Ms. Holmes requested lighter job duties, as her doctor recommended; her request was denied, and she miscarried her child. Ms. Holmes joined a campaign to ensure that all Walmart workers are treated fairly and brought the issue to national attention.[3] In August of 2014, Illinois passed the Illinois Pregnant Workers Fairness Act to protect the health of pregnant working women and their unborn children. This story is all too common— although the federal Pregnancy Discrimination Act requires fair treatment of pregnant workers, courts have interpreted it narrowly, and pregnant women are often forced to choose between the health of their unborn children and the job that will feed those children when they are born.[4]
- *Lilly Ledbetter:* In a now-famous case, Ms. Ledbetter, a nineteen-year employee of Goodyear, learned that she was making thousands of dollars less per year in her job than men who held the same position. Ms. Ledbetter fought the pay discrimination for years in a sex discrimination lawsuit, first winning and then losing on appeal. When her case went to the

Supreme Court, the court ruled that she should have filed her case within 180 days of the first unequal paycheck—something she couldn't possibly have done because she didn't know about the inequality at that time. Ms. Ledbetter continued to fight this discrimination, ultimately winning and helping to establish the Lilly Ledbetter Fair Pay Restoration Act.[5]

- *Lorena Weeks:* Years before Lilly Ledbetter fought pay discrimination at Goodyear, Lorena Weeks fought for the right to work a job as a switchman (someone in charge of keeping equipment running properly) at Southern Bell. Weeks sued Southern Bell for the job, joining forces with a lawyer from the National Organization for Women (NOW). As Gail Collins describes the case in *When Everything Changed*, "*Weeks v. Southern Bell* was one of the first big victories on the road to ending job discrimination against women, a huge cause for celebration at NOW. But for Lorena Weeks herself, it was just another marker in a long and tortuous road."[6] That road did eventually lead to Ms. Weeks getting the job—with back pay for all the years she could have been doing it rather than fighting to do it.

Not having privilege can obviously make you feel powerless, and create a situation in which you must fight those in power for your rights. However, having privilege doesn't necessarily make you feel powerful. Michael Kimmel, in his discussion of the frustration many American men feel when they are told they have privilege, likens the feeling to a "wind chill": "It doesn't matter what the temperature actually is; it only matters how it feels.

Gender equality is felt to be a zero-sum game: if women win, men lose."[7]

This sense that the world should belong to men—that they should "win" in a zero-sum game—is called **entitlement**. Entitlement goes hand-in-hand with privilege—culturally, men are lead to believe that if they can measure up to that all-powerful man we have in our heads, the world is their oyster. When the reality doesn't match the promise, many men believe they are speaking the truth when they say they aren't privileged. Although their frustration is valid, it blinds them to the lived experience of women, who are trying to build lives while receiving the cultural message that they are inferior to men, often in direct and damaging ways. And in one of the deepest ironies of patriarchy, entitlement also obscures the ways in which strict gender norms are harmful to boys and men. (See "Does Sexism Affect Men?" for more information.)

Facing privilege and working toward policies and customs that create equality requires both a belief in your internal power and a hope that you can have external power, at least over your own destiny. Refusing to face it, on the other hand, ensures the status quo.

Do All Women Experience Sexism Identically?

No, women do *not* all experience sexism identically—not by a long shot. Sexism affects women in different ways, according to their backgrounds and characteristics. That's because some women within a patriarchy have privilege—in the form of race, class, sexual identity, physical abilities, or age. Other women do not have privilege, in more ways than one. As Audre Lorde puts it in her essay "Learning from the 60s," "There is no such thing as a single-issue struggle because we do not live single-issue lives."[8]

As you review the terms below, keep in mind that they describe the **lived experience** of particular women—the direct and indirect ways they experience sexism and other forms of discrimination as they go about their daily lives. Much of that sexism is connected to the ways in which a particular woman doesn't "measure up" to an unreachable ideal. We all know what that ideal looks like—the white, thin, gorgeous, rich, heterosexual young woman of our national dreams.

We also all have stereotypes in our heads—we think specific things when we hear "Native American" or "Asian" or "lesbian" or "working class" or "over 50." The experiences of an individual American woman are shaped by who she is in combination with the ways our culture says she doesn't meet the ideal—and the ways she is denied both internal and external power.

Intersectionality

Kimberlé Crenshaw, a UCLA law professor, author, and civil rights activist, coined the term **intersectionality** to discuss the ways in which various forms of discrimination affect the lives of women of color. Intersectionality describes the intersection of racism, sexism, and other forms of discrimination in the lives of many women. This intersection has serious cultural, legal, and financial consequences—both for individual women and for groups of women.

In her work, Crenshaw calls attention to the fact that black women have had to frame their experiences either as "women" (within a political and cultural framework that puts the perspectives, experiences, and needs of white middle-class women at the center) or as "black" (within a political and cultural framework that puts the perspectives, experiences, and needs of black men at the center). Both frameworks leave black women without the means to describe and address their lived experience.

Crenshaw gives concrete examples of the ways in which sexism and racism affect the lives of black women, and the courts' failure to recognize this intersection, in her essay "Demarginalizing the Intersection of Race and Sex." She describes three court cases in which black women faced the consequences of race and sex discrimination, summarized below:[9]

- ***Degraffenreid v. General Motors*:** In this case, five black women sued General Motors for discrimination. GM had hired no black women before 1964; all of the black women hired after 1970 lost their jobs in a seniority-based layoff. The women lost their suit on the basis of sex discrimination: because GM had hired white women before 1964, they recognized no sex discrimination.
- ***Moore v. Hughes Helicopters, Inc.*:** In this case, the plaintiff—Moore—showed evidence that her employer was promoting more men than women to supervisory positions, and that more white men than black men were getting these jobs. The court claimed that Moore couldn't represent all women at Hughes, as she was claiming discrimination "only" as a black woman.
- ***Payne v. Travenol*:** Two black women brought a suit against a pharmaceutical plant on behalf of all black employees; however, the court refused to allow the plaintiffs to represent black men. Although the court

ultimately ruled in favor of the women—finding that there had been race discrimination at the plant—it did not extend the finding to black men.

Each of these cases dealt with race and sex as though they were entirely separate—in some cases, not allowing black women to represent either "women" or "blacks," and in others, not allowing black women to prove sex discrimination simply as "women." Crenshaw asks us to see the whole picture: "Black women sometimes experience discrimination in ways similar to white women's experiences; sometimes they share very similar experiences with Black men. Yet often they experience double-discrimination—the combined effects of practices which discriminate on the basis of race, and on the basis of sex. And sometimes, they experience discrimination as Black women—not the sum of race and sex discrimination, but as Black women."[10]

TYPES OF DISCRIMINATION

Intersectionality plays out differently for different women, according to their characteristics and the forms of discrimination aimed at them. Most of us are familiar with the following forms of discrimination, as they crop up in our national discussions fairly often.

- **_Racism:_** Women of color deal with **racism**, or the belief, institutionalized in laws and customs, that people of color are inferior to white people. Stereotypes are a tool of racism, which means that women of color deal with specific forms of racism—stereotypes that say some women are sexually immoral, some are "princesses," etc.—as they deal with sexism.

- *Homophobia:* Lesbians and bisexual women ⌐ with **homophobia**, or the belief, institutionalized in laws and customs, that homosexuals (and those with other sexual identities that do not conform to traditional gender roles, such as bisexuals) are inferior to heterosexuals, and to be feared and distrusted. Homophobia is connected to **heteronormativity**—the ways in which we treat heterosexuality as "normal" and all other sexual identities as deviant.

There are many other ways in which a patriarchy enforces the idea that some people are better than others:

- *Ableism:* Women with disabilities deal with **ableism**, or the belief, institutionalized in laws and customs, that people with disabilities are inferior to people without disabilities.
- *Ageism:* Older women deal with **ageism**, or the belief, institutionalized in laws and customs, that older people are inferior to younger people.
- *Anti-Semitism:* Jewish women deal with **anti-Semitism**, or the belief, institutionalized in laws and customs, that Jewish people are inferior to Christians, and to be feared and distrusted.
- *Colonialism:* Native American women and women from places the U.S. has colonized (such as Puerto Rico) deal with **colonialism**, or the belief, institutionalized in laws and customs, that groups of people whose land has been conquered—however long ago or recently—are inferior to groups of people who took the land.

- *Colorism:* Women of color deal with **colorism**, or the belief, institutionalized in laws and customs, that those with darker skin are inferior to those with lighter skin. Colorism often plays out within communities of color in which darker-skinned people are discriminated against by lighter-skinned ones. It also plays a role in mainstream culture: for example, most black female celebrities do not have dark skin. This bias against dark skin is why the cultural recognition of Lupita Nyong'o's beauty and talent is so important.
- *Classism:* Working-class and poor women deal with **classism**, or the belief, institutionalized in laws and customs, that those with less money and status are inferior to those with more money and status.
- *Islamophobia:* Muslim women deal with **Islamophobia**, or the belief, institutionalized in laws and customs, that Muslims are inferior to Christians, and to be feared and distrusted.
- *Transphobia:* Transgender and transsexual women deal with **transphobia**, or the belief, institutionalized in laws and customs, that transgender and transsexual people are inferior to those with traditional gender expressions, and to be feared and distrusted.

Women, men, and children who do not fit the "norm" in one or more ways are **marginalized** in our society. Their experiences and perceptions are pushed outside the scope of our lens, whether the "lens" is a movie camera, a news story, or a national list of concerns and needs. Some forms of marginalization are a huge deal when it comes to even the basics of power, like access to health care and education and the ability to make life decisions about marriage, childbirth, and adoption. In addition, some marginalized women—women of color, women who don't conform to sex and gender norms, and women living in poverty—are more likely to be the targets of violence. (See "How is Sexism Connected to Violence?")

Does Sexism Affect Children?

If little girls are made of sugar and spice and everything nice, what are little boys made of? Snips and snails and puppy dog tails, of course. In other words, girls are about sweetness and boys are about playful activity, which requires being dirty and smelly. Here, in the lines of a simple nursery rhyme, is the difference between sex and gender—and the ways that sexism shapes our thoughts about both.

A person's **sex** is determined by biology: males have penises and females have vaginas. A person's **gender** is shaped by our cultural ideas of what it means to be female or male. If you put a girl toddler and a boy toddler in a mud puddle, who splashes happily and who has a tantrum has nothing to do with biology and everything to do with personality and mood. But the concept of gender in the nursery rhyme insists that only boys like to play in the mud, and only girls are kind and gentle. These are two of the main ideas within traditional views of **masculinity**, or gender traits assigned to males, and **femininity**, or gender traits assigned to females.

> **Note:** Biology isn't always clear-cut—for example, intersex people have biological characteristics of both sexes. However, sex always refers to the body, to the external and internal sex organs.

Gender and sex often intersect, and the lines between the two can blur—some people enjoy playing with the lines as part of their sexuality. Gender is deeply connected to how we present ourselves as sexual beings. We make choices about clothing and personal appearance that express how we perceive our own gender. There are lesbians who love a frilly pink skirt and lesbians who would never wear one, just as there are heterosexual women on both sides of that equation.

Gender can also connect to the activities we enjoy—some activities are seen as "male" and some as "female," though the division is a cultural one. There are lesbians who want to bake cookies all day and heterosexual women who want to fix motorcycles all day—and there are heterosexual men who enjoy doing both. If you observe all the people in our culture enjoying a variety of jobs and hobbies, you can see that having a penis or a vagina (or a particular sexual identity) doesn't determine your capabilities or interests. This doesn't mean that biology isn't a factor in shaping who we are—just that biology isn't *the* factor in shaping who we are and what we can do.

Yet traditional notions of masculinity and femininity insist that biology is destiny, and that anyone acting outside strictly defined gender roles is an exception to the rule. These notions are sexist, as they keep traditional power dynamics in place: girls are passive, boys are active, and power (both internal and external) comes when you view yourself as someone who can do stuff.

When sexist ideas are taught to our children—via advertisements, toys, movies, TV shows, and books—they harm the self-esteem of both girls and boys. And kids are being bombarded with sexist messages these days, as Diane Levin and Jean Kilbourne describe in *So Sexy So Soon*: "A narrow definition of femininity and sexuality encourages girls to focus heavily on appearance and sex appeal. They learn at a very young age that their value is determined by how beautiful, thin, 'hot,' and sexy they are. And boys, who get a very narrow definition of masculinity that promotes insensitivity and macho behavior, are taught to judge girls based on how close they come to an artificial, impossible, and shallow ideal."[11]

How Sexism Affects Girls

As Levin and Kilbourne note, our culture is focused on the idea that femininity is about appearance—not just attractiveness but sexiness. Through the media they are steeped in, American girls learn that to be sexually attractive to boys is the most important thing about womanhood. Teaching our kids—boys as well as girls—to view girls in this way is known as **sexualization**.

Sexualization starts in the media and extends to the mall, as the products that are marketed to girls—from Barbies to Bratz dolls to pre-teen clothing—reinforce this message. Although there is nothing wrong with a girl enjoying a tiara, our culture makes it very clear that girls should put on the tiara and never pick up a tool belt.

As the mother of a daughter, I am keenly aware of this issue, and have navigated it from toddlerhood to the early teens. Many of my conversations with my daughter center on building up her sense of internal power and self-ownership. Peggy Orenstein writes about this issue in her book *Cinderella Ate My Daughter*: "Even as new educational and professional opportunities unfurl before my daughter and her peers, so does the path that encourages them to equate identity with image, self-expression with appearance, femininity with performance, pleasure with pleasing, and sexuality with sexualization."[12]

Concern about the effect of sexualization on girls is so great that the American Psychological Association has a task force that has been studying it for years—and proven that sexualization in our media leads to low self-esteem, eating disorders, and other unhealthy consequences for American girls. That's the bad news. The good news is that many people recognize the unhealthy effects of raising our kids on sexist ideas, and are forming organizations and companies that empower, rather than limit, girls.

While many of these organizations recognize that sexism affects boys as well as girls and work to break down stereotypes that limit boys, their primary focus is on the empowerment of girls. This focus is necessary, as in a sexist society it is girls who are told they aren't "good enough" to do the things boys do, or that their only value is in appearance. But boys are the other half of the equation—and they need guidance tailored specifically to them.

How Sexism Affects Boys

The idea that masculinity hurts boys (and men) sounds backwards to many of us—men aren't supposed to be hurt by much of anything, and certainly not by their own manhood. Masculinity simply *is*, we say, and cannot be changed. Then we look at our boys—their poor performance in school, their issues with bullying, their unwillingness to discuss their problems, their high rates of suicide—and we think our half-changed society is to blame, that girls and women seeking achievement and power are to blame. Boys must be boys, and we aren't letting them—so, the logic goes, back up the time machine and let men be men. Then all will be well again.

Not so, according to the people who study the needs of developing men—all those boys who are struggling to understand what it means to be boys, and then men. In his documentary *Tough*

Guise, Jackson Katz speaks to many young men who describe the pressure to be a "real man"—tough, strong, independent, hard, in control. Katz points out that this concept of masculinity puts men and boys into a box—everyone in it is a "real man." The boys on the outside of the box are wusses, wimps, fags, and sissies. The box that defines manhood puts a great deal of pressure on boys to conform.[13] (See "How is Sexism Vital to Traditional Masculinity?")

In *Masterminds and Wingmen,* her book about the pressures and power dynamics of boyhood, Rosalind Wiseman calls this box the Act Like a Man Box, or ALMB. In her work with boys, Wiseman connects the dots between boys' pain and struggles and their need to repress who they are to fit into this narrow definition of manhood: "...these invisible rules convince them what emotions they're allowed to have and how to express them. It stops them from asking for help."[14] Wiseman wants to empower boys to think and grow outside the box.

As the mother of a boy, I am keenly aware of the messages our culture sends boys and the damage these messages can do to him. My conversations with my son center on making sure he knows it is OK to be his full self, to have feelings and express them. I also emphasize that violence doesn't define him as male. Just as our media sexualizes girls, it does much to convince boys that violence is the bedrock of masculinity. As Levin and Kilbourne put it, "The onslaught of violence makes it harder for boys to develop into caring sexual beings capable of having fulfilling and connected relationships. Boys learn harmful messages about the role of violence within relationships and in the wider community. As girls see boys' involvement with violence and boys see girls' involvement with sexiness, they all learn damaging lessons about what to value in themselves and their own gender as well as about one another."[15]

Unfortunately, we don't have many organizations created solely to teach boys that being a man doesn't have to rely on a sexist idea of manhood. As a nation, we need to be listening to the experts on gender, sexuality, and sexism—for our boys' sake as well as our girls'.

How is Sexism Connected to Beauty?

From fairy tales to music videos, from magazines to blockbuster movies, beautiful women—all of them eerily similar, airbrushed to digital perfection—stare at us with vacant eyes and half-open mouths. Women learn we should be like these women— this one incredibly thin and gorgeous woman—no matter how different we may be, in body size and shape, in skin color, in facial features. She is our model of womanhood, and if we fail to meet her impossible standard, we fail at what we have been told, since childhood, is the most important thing we can ever be: beautiful.

If beauty is in the eye of the beholder, why is our media so insistent that only one type of woman—and only a digitally altered version of her—is beautiful? Because in our culture, beauty isn't about beauty at all—it's about power. Naomi Wolf expresses this fact brilliantly in her book *The Beauty Myth*. Wolf describes the beauty myth as an unreachable ideal—one that has existed in different cultures at different times, and held up different standards of beauty, but always as a way to keep women preoccupied with appearance rather than power (both internal and external). Wolf asks us to think about power when we look at images of beauty in culture: "When faced with the myth, the questions to ask are not about women's faces and bodies but about the power relations of the situation. Who is this serving? Who says? Who profits? What is the context?"[16]

Images of beauty in our culture are connected to sexism because they go to the very heart of power—of who defines womanhood, and how. Our cultural images of beauty might portray women, but they do not speak to the humanity of women: instead, they keep women feeling insecure, questioning ourselves and feeling inferior to an unreachable ideal. Beauty is connected to self-esteem, and the beauty myth ensures that women will be unsatisfied with ourselves: "Most urgently, women's identity must be premised upon our 'beauty' so that we will remain vulnerable to outside approval, carrying the vital sensitive organ of self-esteem exposed to the air."[17]

Objectification

Our cultural images of beauty portray women as sexual objects rather than as full human beings with desires and the power to act on those desires. This treatment is known as **objectification**.

Objectification can be hard to identify because we are so surrounded by it that it feels normal. Consider how many advertisements you've seen that show just a part of a woman's body—her breasts, her legs, her rear end. Compartmentalizing women's bodies is at the center of objectification, as it encourages us to stop seeing women as whole beings. When women see ourselves as the media sees us, we are encouraged to **self-objectify**, or to see ourselves not as whole women but as sexual objects: "The questions Whom do I desire? Why? What will I do about it? are turned around: Would I desire myself? Why? Why not? What can I do about it?"[18]

We are becoming more aware of objectification, in no small part because of the work of Jennifer Siebel Newsome, who founded The Representation Project and made the films *Miss Representation* and *The Mask You Live In*. *Miss Representation* reveals the link between female objectification and power, or the lack of it. The film shows images of women being objectified in our media along with statistics about the lack of external power that women hold in our culture. It draws a clear link between the cultural objectification of women, the portrayal of violence against women, and the consequences for female power, both internal and external, in U.S. society.

Objectification has many unhealthy consequences for girls and women, including eating disorders and low self-esteem. These consequences have been well documented in the American Psychological Association's report on the sexualization of girls. (See "How Does Sexism Affect Self-Esteem?" for more information.)

Sexual Agency

Unfortunately, our culture often confuses objectification with **sexual agency** (also known as **sexual empowerment**), or the ability to make decisions about one's own sexuality, from how a person presents her/himself to how she/he handles decisions about sex and reproduction. Sexual agency relies on the power of a person to present herself as a sexual person from the inside out, rather than having sexuality defined from the outside in. Sexual agency can be confused with objectification for a few reasons:

- *The Media:* Women who willingly participate in media that objectifies women often describe themselves as empowered. And indeed an individual woman might feel empowered in a limited sense, even as she is selling the general public a version of sexuality that portrays women as objects—and even as she knows she must conform to a particular standard or pay the price.

- *Miscommunication:* Because our culture objectifies women, it is possible for a woman to wear a dress for herself—because it is a genuine expression of her sense of beauty and of her own, internal sexuality—while the people around her assume she is wearing it for them, either to tease and entice them or to intimidate or shame them. This is the effect our media has on our daily interactions, and the ways in which the connection between sexism and beauty play out in individual lives.

- *Mixed Messages:* It is also possible for a woman to be wearing a dress for several reasons—after all, why do we define beauty and sexiness as we do? A woman might be very conscious of the power that beauty gives her—she is turning heads and starting conversations. Although that power is limited and limiting, she might not see it as such. Or she might be wearing a dress partly for herself and partly for attention from others: such is the nature of human interactions, and of sexuality. And, of course, there is nothing wrong with enjoying the desire of others, or getting a compliment—these are normal and healthy parts of our humanity and our sexuality. Objectification comes into play when a woman and/or the people around her view her as a sexy prop rather than as a person.

When sorting through the questions around objectification, it is helpful to bring it back to power. Ask those questions that Naomi Wolf posed: Who is this serving? Who says? Who profits? When it comes to media, we aren't just thinking about actresses and models in movies and videos and advertisements: behind the scenes are directors and producers and writers and executives, overwhelmingly male, crafting and profiting from the presentation of female sexuality that we see all around us.

MALE OBJECTIFICATION

To a lesser degree than women, men are also objectified in our media, and they too are measured against an unrealistic physical image—the buff and strong counterpart to the thin female ideal. Many men struggle with this ideal and suffer the consequences, including eating disorders and low self-esteem.[19] And the "ideal" male body isn't only muscular and fit: our culture defines a "real" man as well-endowed. As Susan Bordo puts it in *The Male Body*, "The humongous penis, like the idealized female body, is a cultural fantasy."[20]

As Bordo discusses, there is a long history of male body imagery—including the penis, emphasized in underwear ads and on display in porn—in our culture, both in connection with traditional masculinity and with playing to the gaze of gay men. And our preoccupation isn't only with the actual penis—much of our imagery is about the phallus, or the symbolic penis, which we encounter in countless ads and movies. Bordo discusses the impact of the phallus on the male psyche: "The phallus is a cultural icon which men are taught to aspire to. They cannot succeed. Young men...have trouble seeing their penises realistically, and consistently judge them to be smaller than they actually are. In part, that's because it's not really flesh-and-blood penises that shape a young man's perception that his penis is less than it is or should be, but a majestic imaginary member, against which no man's penis can ever measure up."[21]

> **Note:** *Although some of this imagery is aimed at gay men, our culture defines a "masculine" man as heterosexual, and male attractiveness as a tool to "get" a beautiful woman. In addition, male beauty—or the cultivation of it—is sometimes seen as "feminine," and used as fuel for homophobia.*

While male objectification is similar to female objectification in many ways, a patriarchy doesn't define male beauty as the basis for all male power, and men in most professions are not prevented from holding power on the basis of beauty. There are many cases—cited in both *The Beauty Myth* and in Susan Faludi's *Backlash*—in which women have lost jobs because they were not considered "beautiful" enough or they were considered "too beautiful."

How is Sexism Vital
to Traditional Masculinity?

Most of us can rattle off the characteristics a "real man" is supposed to have—muscular, tough (emotionally and physically—able to fight and win), good-looking, rich, daring, and popular with the ladies. This set of characteristics makes up our cultural understanding of masculinity. Although most of us wouldn't list "not a woman—because women are weak and emotional and not as awesome as men," or "not a gay man—because gay men are like women," we have an understanding that a masculine man is definitely and always NOT a woman and NOT homosexual, and that the idea he might be either one is an insult to his manhood.

Men insult each other with words that imply either womanliness or homosexuality as a way to prove their masculinity on a regular basis—sometimes these insults are said in earnest, sometimes jokingly as a form of male bonding. In both cases, the words—pussy, girl, fag, wimp—aren't really about women or gay men. They are about masculinity, and the need to prove it.

Using Sexism to Prove Masculinity

You run like a girl, or throw like a girl. You like to play with dolls, and you're going home to cry to your mama, you mama's boy. When boys get a little older, the words change—you're a pussy. Or, you get a lot of pussy—hos and sluts are begging you for it. Bitches can't keep their hands off you.

These are the kinds of things boys learn to use as proof of manhood, and grown men use to bolster their masculinity in the eyes of other men. The statements are blatantly sexist—girls can't run or throw as well as boys, vaginas are symbols of weakness, and women who have sex with men are checkmarks on a masculine scoreboard. Although boys and men are taught to say these things to each other, they are also taught that they shouldn't be mean to girls, that women are supposed to be their equals at school, in the workforce, and at home, and that using a woman for sex isn't something "nice guys" do. In other words, men get mixed messages about women—they should respect us to our faces and disrespect us behind our backs. Sexism is supposed to be a masculine secret, and we use four words to keep a lid on it: boys will be boys.

Many men who don't consciously hold sexist beliefs will use sexism to prove their masculinity—they might feel bad about it, but they know this is the way the game is played, and they know their masculinity is on the line. Or, if they don't actively use sexism, they don't point it out when other men are using it. They just laugh uncomfortably and wait for it to be over. Jackson Katz discusses the discomfort of nonsexist men—and the isolation they can feel—in *The Macho Paradox:* "There have been a number of studies in the past several years that demonstrate that significant numbers of men are uncomfortable with the way some of their male peers talk about and treat women. But since few men in our society have dared to talk publically about such matters, many men think they are the only ones who feel uncomfortable."[22]

Many men who make sexist comments aren't doing so uncomfortably—on the contrary, they truly believe women are inferior, and they will get nasty with their sexism. When sexism takes this obvious, hateful form, it's called misogyny. **Misogyny**—woman-hating—makes a patriarchy stronger, as it reinforces every sexist policy and practice with the idea that women aren't only inferior, we are worthy of contempt and all kinds of pain, and deserve no dignity. Misogyny is directly linked to violence against women, as it condones the idea that men should hurt, rape, and even kill women. (For more information, see "How is Sexism Connected to Violence?")

> *Note:* *Transgender and transsexual women deal with* **transmisogyny**, *a term author Julia Serano introduced in her book Whipping Girl. Transmisogny is hatred aimed at trans women who are expressing their femaleness or femininity.*

Using Homophobia to Prove Masculinity

As Michael Kimmel states in "Masculinity as Homophobia," "Homophobia and sexism go hand in hand."[23] Why? Because to prove "real" manhood, traditional masculinity requires men to say that gay men are like women, who are inferior to men. As the name homophobia implies, the need to prove one's masculinity as not feminine or weak is based in fear. A fear of being powerless, of being dominated by other men, of being exposed as a fraud. Kimmel gives voice to this fear: "Our fear is the fear of humiliation. We are ashamed to be afraid."[24]

Note: *It is important to recognize the difference between masculinity and men themselves. Many men are pushing back against a rigidly defined masculinity that limits them as human beings and hurts other people.*

Masculinity and Power

As we consider how masculinity is related to sexism, it's important to remember that sexism is about both external and internal power. Our traditional definition of masculinity—which relies on sexism as proof of manhood—establishes the power of some men in our society. As Michael Kimmel puts it, "We equate manhood with being strong, successful, capable, reliable, in control. The very definitions of manhood we have developed in our culture maintain the power that some men have over other men and that men have over women."[25] In other words, traditional masculinity supports—and in many ways is at the root of—patriarchy.

How Does Sexism Affect Self-Esteem?

I love Watty Piper's *The Little Engine That Could.* I loved it as a kid, and I loved reading it to my kids as a mom. Who wouldn't be into its message: "*I think I can, I think I can, I think I can…,*" says the Little Engine as she chugs up the huge mountain that she is afraid she can't handle. And "*I thought I could, I thought I could, I thought I could…,*" she says on her way down. We all want that feeling that the Little Engine has after making it up the mountain—we all deserve that feeling, after hard work leads to an accomplishment.

But before we can claim an accomplishment, we must believe it's possible—*I think I can* comes before *I thought I could*. And belief in oneself doesn't only apply to accomplishment in the external world—it goes to our very core, our ability to be our best selves. As Gloria Steinem puts it in *Revolution from Within*, "Believing in a true self is what allows a true self to be born."[26] This belief in a true self, and our ability to act on that belief and see that our true self matters to the world around us, is **self-esteem**. It is entwined with both internal and external power, and it is vital to the well-being of each and every one of us.

Sexism, with its constant cultural messages that girls and women are tools for male conquest and power, and its legal and cultural barriers to female accomplishment, gets in the way of that true self—for both females and males.

Sexism, Self-Esteem, and Females

We recognize as a society that if an individual person—a parent or a teacher or a peer—yells something like, "You no-good slut!" or "You can't do math, run, use computers, play the best games, or be the leader—so just sit there, shut up, and look pretty!" that person is being verbally abusive. Sexism bullies and verbally abuses American women and girls all day every day, but because it is often cultural and not directly personal, we don't see or name sexism for what it is. (Even when it is directly personal, our culture affirms it—so we still don't always name it.) Sexism deeply affects the self-esteem—the sense of internal power that could lead to external power—in girls and women.

When you are repeatedly told you are less than, no good, dumb, silly, superficial, wrong or bad or dirty, it gets into your head. It gets into your heart. It goes right to the foundation of who you think you are and what you think you can do. Studies back up this link between the sexist treatment of girls and women and self-esteem. The American Psychological Association has studied the effect of our culture's sexualization of girls—teaching girls that objectification is their path to power, both internal and external— for several years. Here's some wisdom from their 2007 report (reprinted in 2010):

> Just at the time when girls begin to construct identity, they are more likely to suffer losses in self-esteem. Research has documented losses in self-esteem for girls in adolescence (e.g., Harter, 1998; Major, Barr, & Zubek, 1999), and perceived physical attractiveness is closely linked to self-esteem (Polce-Lynch, Myers, & Kilmartin, 1998). In particular, Tolman, Impett, Tracy, and Michael (2006) have shown that in the eighth grade, girls who objectify their bodies more have much lower self-esteem. For this reason, diminishing self esteem arising in early adolescence may make girls particularly vulnerable to cultural messages that promise them popularity, effectiveness, and social acceptance through the right "sexy" look.[27]

There are many books that prove and analyze the link between sexism and self-esteem and the consequences for females, such as Naomi Wolf's *The Beauty Myth* and Susan Bordo's *Unbearable Weight* and Jean Kilbourne and Diane Levin's *So Sexy So Soon*. There are also many organizations that study this link, like the Women's Media Center and The Representation Project and The Geena Davis Institute on Gender and Media. Despite this body of evidence and the people working to raise cultural awareness of it, we have trouble recognizing sexism and drawing the line when it comes to female self-esteem. Our failure to do so demonstrates how deeply sexism is embedded in our society.

FEMALE CHOICE

In an article for *The Daily Beast* in February 2014, Christina Hoff Sommers claimed that the wage gap is bogus because it is due, in part, to sex segregation within the workforce (e.g., there are more female teachers and secretaries than female engineers and doctors). Ms. Sommers points out that women are choosing their jobs, and asserts that the American Association of University Women's claim that women's choices are influenced by cultural messages—by sexism—is itself sexist: "To say that these women remain helplessly in thrall to sexist stereotypes, and manipulated into life choices by forces beyond their control, is divorced from reality—and demeaning to boot."[28]

I get why Ms. Sommers would say this—to say that sexism gets in your head might make it sound like women are weak, like we just can't overcome the stuff we hear and see and turn "You're bad at math!" into "I think I can!" all by ourselves. And it would be lovely to think that each woman, alone, could fight the barrage of messages in her head and heart and make choices completely separate from what she hears and sees around her—in other words, her self-esteem is strong enough, despite being under fire since childhood, to overcome external messages. But even if that were the case for most women (as it has clearly been for some— otherwise we'd have no success stories at all), external barriers are part of the uneven playing field. Here, external power matters as much as internal power, and sexism influences both.

SELF-CRITICISM

In *The End of Men*, Hanna Rosin discusses a female Wall Street executive who explains the reaction that both men and women have when a woman is assertive at work. The executive, Sallie Krawcheck, doesn't see this reaction as sexist or biased, but as an automatic response. She calls this response The Twitch, "...the instinctive wince we do when a woman unsheathes her sword."[29]

That wince *is* bias. It is sexism—an internalized attitude that says women shouldn't be assertive about our own needs and desires. Sheryl Sandberg discusses this sexism in *Lean In*, advising women to accommodate it in just the right way, because that's the world we live in. Indeed, that is the world we live in—not just outside our own minds and bodies, but inside ourselves. When I say that sexism—and racism, which hits women of color with a double-whammy, and classism, which hits poor women of color with a triple-whammy—is unconscious and internal, this is what I mean. We have learned to put ourselves down, and not to call the put-down by its name. (For more information on women and sexism, see "Can Women Be Sexist?")

Trying to believe in your internal power and your ability to have external power as a female in a patriarchy is like being The Little Engine that Could with a chorus of hecklers by the side of the track. You have to stick your fingers in your ears and make your *I think I can* louder than their *Oh no you don't*—and often, even with your fingers in your ears, you hear *Oh no you don't* over and over.

Sexism, Self-Esteem, and Males

For men, sexism can seemingly boost self-esteem—if women are inferior, men are superior. Sexism is a tool in proving masculinity, which is linked to self-esteem for men. However, any self-esteem built on putting another person down is unstable and ultimately futile—for true self-esteem must come from within.

When a man degrades a woman to score points with h buddies and appear more masculine, he is going to get some laughs and some praise. But the praise will be a quick fix that needs to be repeated over and over. If, on the other hand, he draws on his own reserves, his unique worth, for self-esteem, relying on sexism (as well as racism and homophobia) to make himself feel more masculine is unnecessary. However, if he feels unsure of his unique worth, the temptation to create a sense of superiority will be strong—and highly encouraged by our culture.

In a patriarchy, the male dependence on female inferiority for self-esteem creates an unhealthy dynamic that we see played out in a million ways. Boys and men are taught to say, "I'm smart, strong, cool and capable because they're not." And if the "...they're not" goes away, then what?

"Who am I—am I OK?" This is the silent question staring boys and men in the face. And the answer for boys and men, as for girls and women, must be a resounding YES. You are OK, just as you are—you are unique, and valued for your true self.

Can Women Be Sexist?

As I discussed in "How Does Sexism Affect Self Esteem?" sexism is internalized—it gets into everyone's heads, because we live in a sexist culture. This internalization means sexist ideas and practices don't only come from men—women can also be sexist.

However, our national conversations tend to ignore or refute female sexism. In the newspaper and on talk shows, people often assume that if a woman participates in an activity or makes a statement or supports a policy, her sex makes her judgments and actions empowering to women, or at least not harmful to women. The assumption is: if a woman does or says it, it must not be sexist. For example, in an April 2014 article for *The Washington Post*, George Will claimed that former Michigan Secretary of State Terri Lynn Land "...represents Republicans' most effective response to Democrats' hyperventilating about the 'war on women'—female candidates."[30]

This assumption that female support automatically makes a policy or belief good for women allows some women to participate in sexist practices or express sexist ideas—in other words, to support patriarchy—in the name of female empowerment. Other women support patriarchy not as upholders of women, but as female defenders of traditional masculinity. And some women support patriarchy by using violence against others—their male partners, their children, or other women.

Female Chauvinist Pigs

In *The End of Men*, Hanna Rosin describes young businesswomen who take sexism in stride. As the women gather at a bar with men their age—some boyfriends, some friends—they barely register a cell phone picture of a woman performing fellatio on a snowman that the guys are snickering over. As Rosin puts it, "This was their way of psyching the men out, by refusing to back down in any game where, in another era, they would have been assumed to be the weaker opponent."[31] Here, young women are playing a male game by what appear to be their own rules, as they chart a path to the top of their careers: "In general, their response was not to call in the lawyers, but to rise—or maybe stoop—to the occasion."[32] Why would they do such a thing? According to Rosin, it's about power: "Instead of being done in by a highly sexualized culture, women are learning to manipulate it to their advantage."[33]

And she's right—these women are getting where they want go, using sex as a tool, often breaking their own hearts as well as the hearts of men who fall in love with them. The fact that they've figured out how to game the system doesn't mean sexism is gone—and Rosin doesn't claim it does. But it also doesn't mean the women have claimed the internal power necessary to set the terms of their external power.

These women are playing the games of patriarchy by becoming what journalist Ariel Levy calls Female Chauvinist Pigs, in her book of the same name: "If Male Chauvinist Pigs were men who regarded women as pieces of meat, we would outdo them and be Female Chauvinist Pigs, women who make sex objects of other women and of ourselves."[34]

These women have some external power—they are making good money, advancing their careers, living their lives on their own terms to a large degree. But they rely on sexism to do so. Levy describes why this is a problem, and why it keeps a patriarchy alive: "There's just one thing: Even if you are a woman who achieves the ultimate and becomes like a man, you will still always be like a woman. And as long as womanhood is thought of as something to escape from, something less than manhood, you will be thought less of, too."[35]

Defenders of Traditional Masculinity

Many women who support patriarchy do so as defenders of men as well as women—but only in the name of traditional gender roles. These women—Phyllis Schlafly and her niece, Suzanne Venker, Camille Paglia, and Christinia Hoff Sommers, to name a few—speak of the loss of male power, concern about boys' issues, and what they see as a cultural need for traditional masculinity. Here are two of their regular arguments:

- ***The War on Men:*** In her November 2012 article for
  Fox News, "The war on men," Suzanne Venker
  claims that young women are having trouble finding
  mates because we've abandoned traditional gender
  roles: "Men want to love women, not compete with
  them. They want to provide for and protect their
  families—it's in their DNA. But modern women
  won't let them."[36]
- ***It's a Man's World:*** In a December 2013 article for
  Time, Camille Paglia defends men in the name of
  traditional masculinity: "When an educated culture
  routinely denigrates masculinity and manhood, then
  women will be perpetually stuck with boys, who have
  no incentive to mature or to honor their
  commitments."[37]

You get the idea, and you've heard it often. Men must be men,
women must be women: heterosexually-defined biology is
destiny, and to pretend otherwise is to bring about our ruination.
And the idea that sex is separate from gender, or men are separate
from masculinity and women separate from femininity? Academic
hogwash.

These ideas support patriarchy—upheld by traditional
masculinity, which relies on sexism—wholeheartedly in the name
of happiness, for women as well as men, girls as well as boys. I
have no doubt that women who support patriarchy have genuine
concern for men and boys, but as they argue for traditional
masculinity, they miss the ways in which it hurts males—the
statements made by boys themselves in *Masterminds and
Wingmen* that I discussed in "Does Sexism Affect Children?"

Violence against Others

Women can be cruel enforcers of patriarchy on a personal level by abusing men, other women, and children. In *Feminism is for Everybody,* bell hooks points out that women who are violent to their children enforce the idea that violence is an acceptable method of control—that a dominant party (a parent) can hold her or his position over a party with less power (a child) via violence.[38]

This is an important point because it shifts our thinking from "only men do violence" (and many do, in greater numbers than women) to "patriarchy requires violence for its survival." The issue at the center of a sexist society, then, is not "women vs. men"—it is patriarchy, enforced via violence or the threat of violence.

This fact is evident when we consider the verbal violence women can and sometimes do use against one another and against their female children—slut, whore, bitch. Those insults are all rooted in sexism, and they are not always spoken by a man. And when a woman uses violence against her partner (of any gender), she is enforcing the idea, fundamental to a patriarchy, that people have and keep power in a relationship by force.

How Does Sexist Humor Work?

Much of our national conversation about sexism is connected to humor. When is it sexism and when is it a joke? We tend to have trouble making the distinction because we've been taught that sexism is funny.

One of the major ways that men prove their masculinity is by joking with each other—and increasingly, with women—about women's bodies and minds. In other words, men use sexist humor to prove their masculinity to one another. Our media is very aware of this practice, mocking it even while taking it seriously. Barney Stinson on *How I Met Your Mother* was aware of his sexism, making fun of it with his male and female friends even as he reveled in it; first Beavis and Butthead and then the guys on *The Man Show* just couldn't stop giggling about breasts; and Howard Stern is downright nasty in his assessments of the female body, which his audience finds amusing. In public and in private, sexist humor is a tool of patriarchy, a way to convince us all that men are superior and deserve more power, and women are inferior and deserve to serve and entertain men.

While some in our media—like Howard Stern—make sexist statements boldly and crassly, other forms of sexism are more subtle, and therefore more difficult to define. We tend to justify sexist humor with two unconscious ideas: *if we're laughing, it can't be sexist* and *it's funny 'cause it's true.* We also keep sexist humor alive by telling any woman who calls it out that she is taking herself too seriously.

If We're Laughing, It Can't Be Sexist

One way we keep sexist humor alive is by thinking that if it's funny and we laugh, it can't be sexist—especially if a woman is laughing, or willingly part of the joke. We know that sexism is bad and mean—most companies don't want to be seen as sexist, and most people wouldn't walk around saying, "I'm sexist and proud of it!" So, if we laugh at something and someone says it's sexist, well—the someone (almost always a woman, or a group of women) must be wrong. Because laughing at sexism is insensitive, and most of us aren't purposely, consciously insensitive people.

This is why the work of purging sexism is internal—we have to excavate it, to understand that we can see something as funny, not be consciously sexist, and yet still be laughing at a sexist joke.

It's Funny 'Cause It's True

Sometimes Homer Simpson laughs and laughs, and when he's done, he wipes his eyes and says contentedly, "It's funny 'cause it's true." Many of us take this approach to sexism, although we don't see it that way—the sexism is so ingrained in our society, and in our ideas of what it means to be male or female, that we simply laugh. But we are laughing because we think the joke holds truth.

The 2014 Emmys provided a national example of a sexist joke—and a way to understand both why some people might have found it amusing and why it's sexist.

SOFIA VERGARA AT THE EMMYS

During the 2014 Emmys, Sofia Vergara stood atop a rotating pedestal, her body on display like a living, smiling, gorgeous trophy—the comparison easy to make at an awards show. As her body rotated, Television Academy chairman Bruce Rosenblum spoke in the background. When several people called out the bit as sexist, Vergara responded by saying they needed to lighten up: "It means that somebody can be hot and also be funny and make fun of herself."[39]

So—if we put a woman on a rotating pedestal at an awards show, is it sexist or funny? And if a woman refused to get on that pedestal, what would she be—not hot, not funny, not able to make fun of herself? Or simply the kind of woman who doesn't like to be part of sexist jokes?

Some might find the joke "funny 'cause it's true." We do put some women (usually white, always upper- or middle-class) on a pedestal. And we do think hot women are more interesting than men in suits saying boring things. That's the surface of the gag, but it goes deeper—if women are on a pedestal, they aren't behind the camera, or being the president of the Academy. They don't even want to be, because they like it up there in the turning spotlight. *It's funny 'cause it's true* says women want to be on display and nothing more—and men want to watch, while also holding the external power, the money and the terms of our interactions.

If it's harmless fun to imagine a woman as a trophy, then we're free to imagine all women as trophies—especially beautiful women in the entertainment industry, who are often on display in one way or another. And if women are trophies, they aren't movers and shakers—they're safely in one spot, keeping their internal and external power confined to a very narrow conception of beauty and purpose. That's always been the function of that pedestal some of us are said to be on—to provide a perch that defines the scope of our power.

Does that mean there are no perks to the pedestal, or that no woman would ever want to be on it? Absolutely not. The pedestal has its appeal—its form of power, and its glamour. But the power it offers is limited, its glamour rigidly defined: to stay on it, you must depend on the approval of others. Your internal power is defined by an external gaze—a tricky proposition at best, and one that cannot be sustained for the long term, no matter how hard you might try. The woman on a literal pedestal is an excellent example of objectification, discussed in the topic "How is Sexism Connected to Beauty?"

Only Uptight Women Aren't Laughing

Sofia Vergara told women calling out sexism about her bit on the Emmys to "lighten up," and I have heard the same thing when pointing out sexism—that's the standard response. The idea is that women who speak out against sexism can't take a joke. The jokes are riffing on *it's funny 'cause it's true*—so it's just a bit __ ribbing, no harm, no foul.

But sexism—even sexist humor—isn't only, or even primarily, about getting laughs. It's about power. If Sofia Vergara's right, then nothing has to change. If sexism is funny once, it's funny every time and in every context. We don't have to stop doing anything we're doing, from posting jokes about rape on Facebook (there are many memes that make light of and encourage rape, allowed to remain on Facebook because they are posted in the name of humor) to telling female journalists or actresses they're too old to be on TV to joking on *Fox News* that men need to be sure to beat women off camera. On the other hand, if a joke is recognized as sexist, it's time to stop making it—on Facebook, on *Fox News*, at work, at home—everywhere. It's time to change how we talk to each other, and how we view women.

To say that a woman who speaks out against sexism is uptight (and I bet you know what else—ugly, doesn't like sex or can't get any, jealous of younger women, a lesbian—that one gets in some homophobia with your sexism) keeps sexist practices and policies in place. To avoid appearing humorless or uptight, women often play along with sexist humor, agreeing that the joke's on us and it really is funny that our patriarchy dresses up disrespect as humor.

When we admit that it is sexist to imagine a woman as a trophy—even if we think it's funny—it's time to connect the dots between our images of women in the media, the self-esteem issues of girls and women, and the lack of women in positions of power—presidents, chair people, writers, CEOs, directors—in Hollywood and beyond.

How is Sexism Connected to Violence?

When the celebrity website TMZ released a video of Ray Rice beating then-fiancée Janay Palmer unconscious in an elevator, many people were shocked by the beating itself and by the National Football League's (NFL's) lenient response. Beating women is wrong—it goes against the code of honorable masculinity. We all know that.

Ah, but we also all know something else: a "real man" uses violence to establish and maintain power. When you put the violence at the center of traditional masculinity together with sexism, you get a very powerful tool of patriarchy: violence against women. We are a society that condones and even encourages violence against women as a way of establishing and maintaining male power—so much so that we have normalized it.

Sexual Violence

Much of the violence that drives traditional masculinity is linked with sex. As Riane Eisler describes in *Sacred Pleasure*, we are taught to see sexual violence as both abnormal and normal: "On the one hand, the association of sex and violent domination is said not to exist except in the case of just a few perverts. On the other hand, this same association is said to be not only normal but inevitable—just part of human, or more specifically, male nature."[40]

The idea that sexual violence is a part of male nature is closely linked to the idea that female sexuality is dangerous, and must be controlled. These ideas show up in many places, from the lyrics in pop music to gender roles in the movies to the questions we ask a rape victim to the way we prosecute—or fail to prosecute—rape in the military. When a culture considers men to be naturally sexually violent, external male power is preserved at the cost of both external and internal female power. As Jackson Katz puts it in *The Macho Paradox*, "Sexual violence, in short, is part of a broader cultural pattern in which masculinity comes to be linked with power and control over women."[41]

Our national understanding—and definition—of rape and sexual assault have changed over time as a result of women asserting their right to self-ownership and to determine when and with whom they want to have sex. When we discuss rape and sexual assault, it is important to remember that we are discussing crimes with legal definitions and legal consequences—and that those crimes take place within a culture that objectifies women and presents rape as a normal consequence of masculinity. As we seek to understand sexual violence, it is helpful to understand the terms below.

> *Note: Because rape and sexual assault are terms with legal consequences, they have legal definitions—I have taken the definitions of these two terms from the Bureau of Justice Statistics.[42] The Rape, Abuse, and Incest National Network (RAINN) emphasizes that the legal definitions of rape and sexual assault vary by state and maintains a State Law Database.[43]*

- *Rape:* Forced sexual intercourse including psychological coercion as well as physical force. Forced sexual intercourse means vaginal, anal, or oral penetration by the offender(s). Also includes penetration by a foreign object, such as a bottle. Includes attempted rapes, male as well as female victims, and both heterosexual and same sex rape. Attempted rape includes verbal threats of rape.

- ***Sexual Assault:*** A wide range of victimizations, separate from rape or attempted rape. These crimes include attacks or attempted attacks generally involving unwanted sexual contact between victim and offender. Sexual assaults may or may not involve force and include such things as grabbing or fondling. Sexual assault also includes verbal threats.

- ***Consent:*** Voluntary, positive, clearly communicated agreement to participate in sexual activity. A person who is asleep cannot give consent. A person who is mentally or physically incapacitated, due to drugs or alcohol or for any other reason, cannot give consent.[44]

- ***Rape Culture:*** The aspects of our culture that normalize rape and sexual assault, such as movies or song lyrics that glorify sexual violence and interrogations that place blame on victims.

- ***Victim Blaming:*** The practice of questioning a victim's behavior and dress, either implying or stating directly that the victim, rather than the perpetrator, was responsible for the crime.

- ***Intimate Partner Violence (IPV):*** The Centers for Disease Control and Prevention (CDC), which conducts surveys about IPV, defines it as "...physical violence, sexual violence, stalking and psychological aggression (including coercive acts) by a current or former intimate partner."[45] There are four main types of IPV: physical violence, sexual violence, stalking, and psychological aggression.[46]

GENERAL STATISTICS

All women are taught to fear rape—it is a very real threat, and we are given many pointers for avoiding it, from carrying our keys pointed outward as we walk to our cars to keeping our drinks with us at all times when we are at a party. Most of the tips we are given assume that rapists are "out there," lurking in the bushes and waiting to pounce. While some rapes and sexual assaults do happen this way, most do not:

- Approximately 4/5 of assaults are committed by someone known to the victim.[47]
- Approximately 19% of women will be sexually assaulted while in college.[48]
- In 2010, 241 males and 1095 females were murdered by an intimate partner.[49]
- In 2014, approximately 20,300 active-duty U.S. military personnel reported experiencing a sexual assault within the last year. Ninety percent of the assaults took place within a military setting or were perpetrated by military personnel.[50]

PATRIARCHY, VIOLENCE, AND INTERSECTIONALITY

In the topic "Does Sexism Affect All Women Identically?" I discussed intersectionality, or the ways in which different forms of discrimination intersect in the lives of many women. I've also discussed power throughout this book—the ways in which sexism impacts the lives of women via policies and practices. The effects of intersectionality deeply impact marginalized women who are victims of intimate partner violence and sexual violence:

- ***Multi-Racial Women:*** An estimated 32.3% of multiracial women are raped in their lifetimes.[51]
- ***Native American Women:*** Thirty-four percent of American Indian/Alaska Native women will be raped in their lifetimes.[52] Native American

women are twice as likely to be raped or sexually assaulted than women of other races.[53] The majority of the perpetrators of these crimes (an average of 67 percent) are non-Native men.[54] Despite the prevalence of violence against Native women, our national media does not give crimes against them the same focus and attention it gives crimes against white women: this marginalization, in combination with stereotypes of both Native women and men, contributes to a culture in which Native women are seen as expendable (a consequence of colonialism).

- *Black Women:* An estimated 21.2% of black women have been raped in their lifetimes, and 41.2% of black women have experienced physical violence by an intimate partner in their lifetimes.[55] As bell hooks points out in *Ain't I a Woman*, the stereotype that black women are sexually loose—and available for the taking—has its roots in slavery, and continues to influence our culture. Hooks asserts that the rape of enslaved black women "...led to a devaluation of black womanhood that permeated the psyches of all Americans and shaped the social status of all black women once slavery ended."[56] The stereotype of the sexually available black woman, still prevalent today (as evident in countless music videos), impacts how we see black women, and how we treat them when they are victims of rape and assault.

VIOLENCE, LEGAL INSTITUTIONS, AND MARGINALIZED WOMEN

As you can see, women of color are at high risk for sexual violence and intimate partner violence. Our cultural and legal systems often re-victimize these women by:

- *Condoning Violence:* Our media and institutions often condone, excuse, or downplay violence against women. The NFL's responses to intimate partner violence fall under this category, as players who abuse their partners have often been given a mere slap on the wrist.

- *Victim Blaming:* Using the tactics of victim blaming to focus on the victims' behavior rather than the perpetrators' behavior. The #WhyIStayed Twitter campaign, pushing back against public focus on Janay Rice's choices rather than Ray Rice's behavior, pointed out the victim blaming in that situation.

- *Perpetuating Violence:* Allowing or perpetrating violence against women. Some police officers and prison guards use their positions of power to abuse and assault marginalized women. When marginalized women are victims of state violence, the perpetrators are often not punished, or punished very lightly, and gain a good deal of public support. These cases often aren't covered in the mainstream media, or they are downplayed. Examples include Officer Sergeant James B. Johnson (a former guard at the Kentucky

Correctional Institute for Women who was charged with 25 counts of sexual abuse and served no prison time)[57] and Daniel Holtzclaw (an Oklahoma City police officer charged with raping and sexually assaulting several black women while on duty, who had an online support system that raised thousands of dollars).[58] In January of 2016, Holtzclaw was sentenced to 263 years in prison—by the time of his conviction, the case was being covered in the mainstream media,[59] but the rapes and trial were largely passed over or diminished by the major news outlets until then.[60] To get regular updates about news relating to violence against women of color, you must find sources like *Indian Country Today*, *The Root,* and *Colorlines*, because the major news networks, newspapers, and magazines simply do not focus on their stories.

• ***Punishing Self-Defense:*** Punishing victims legally for attempting to protect themselves. Marissa Alexander's case is a recent example of this treatment. Marissa, who fired a warning shot in self-defense against her estranged abusive husband, was sentenced to 20 years in prison, and prosecutors sought to make it 60 years. The group Free Marissa Now worked to counteract this injustice.[61]

When we focus on increased law enforcement and imprisonment as the sole solution to violence against women, we perpetuate these problems. As Victoria Law explains in an October 2014 article for *Truthout*, this approach "...ignores the ways in which race, class, gender identity, and immigration status leave certain women more vulnerable to violence and that greater criminalization often places these same women at risk of state violence."[62]

Does Sexism Influence Religion?

People of all faiths take religion very seriously: it shapes our approach to life, our values. It informs how we think and act as daughters, mothers, fathers, sons, neighbors, citizens. Because religion is the foundation of a believer's connection to God, stating that sexism influences religion can make us uncomfortable. Yet, fairly regularly, we hear religious politicians making sexist—even misogynistic—comments, often about birth control, pregnancy, rape, or abortion. Many Christians in positions of power have made it very clear: they don't think women should have sex for pleasure, use birth control, prosecute rapists, or have legal abortions. Why is it that these statements are coming from Christian men who have power or are seeking it? Are these guys just out of touch—something that has certainly been said about Todd Akin (who claimed a woman couldn't get pregnant from rape, and later spoke of "legitimate rape"),[63] Rick Santorum, and others—or is something else going on?

As we seek to understand the connection between religion and sexism, it's important to keep in mind that sexism is the basis for a patriarchy, and that we live in a patriarchy. Most faiths have elements of patriarchy in them because they were founded thousands of years ago in societies that viewed and treated women as sexual and economic property.

Most American political debates about women are driven by patriarchal (sexist) interpretations of and approaches to Christianity. That doesn't mean that all of the Christians who want to create and enforce policies that keep patriarchy in place are consciously sexist (though some are). It simply means that Christianity—which is the dominant religion in America—can be interpreted through a patriarchal lens, and that there are many people in power who use a sexist version of Christianity as the basis for our laws and customs. Christianity—like all religions—can also be interpreted through a non-patriarchal lens, and many Christians (myself included) are doing just that.

How Does Sexism Degrade

Female Sexuality?

In her book *The Dance of the Dissident Daughter*, Sue Monk Kidd relates a pivotal event in her feminist spiritual awakening. She was in a grocery store with her teenage daughter, shopping a couple of aisles over. When she returned to the aisle where her daughter was, she saw her kneeling on the ground, looking at an item on a lower shelf. Two grown men were nearby, and one nudged the other and said, "Now that's how I like to see a woman—on her knees."[64]

The author describes how she felt: "I stared at my daughter on her knees before these men and could not look away. Somehow she seemed more than my daughter; she was my mother, my grandmother, and myself. She was every woman ever born, bent and contained in a small, ageless cameo, that bore the truth about 'a woman's place.'"[65]

This place is defined as one of service—not always sexual service, but that is definitely part of the deal. And in this deal, sex is understood to be dirty, and to make a woman "less than." If she actually wants the sex or seeks pleasure in it, she is a slut, a whore: she is utterly disposable. The idea that sex is fundamentally dirty and women who like or want it are fundamentally flawed—indeed, the cause of most trouble in this world—has its roots in patriarchal views of religion.

> **Note:** This way of viewing sex is heteronormative, as it assumes all valid sex is heterosexual. As a result, lesbians, bisexual women, and those with other sexual identities are marginalized by this view of sex: their entire sexual identity becomes just another way to view sex as dirty, and women as tainted.

Most women have our own version of Ms. Kidd's story, of her daughter's story. Many of us have more than one. The longer we live, the more we collect, though the stories slowly change as we age. Often, these daily experiences with sexism have sex—and the idea that a woman is degraded by it—at their core.

Experiences with sexism are also connected to a cultural sense of entitlement about women's bodies: the idea, both conscious and unconscious, that female bodies are public property, and it is OK, perhaps even complimentary, to publically comment on them, evaluate them, and touch them. In other words, women shouldn't be able to set boundaries around our bodies, or to set the terms of how we view, speak about, or engage in sex and its consequences. (This idea is at the center of rape culture.) We do have laws against violating sexual boundaries, but the laws are relatively recent in our culture, and we have many cultural practices that contradict them.

Sexual Harassment

One of the most important laws we have around sexual boundaries protects both women and men from sexual harassment in the workplace. The U.S. Equal Employment Opportunity Commission (EEOC) states that sexual harassment is "...a form of sex discrimination that violates Title VII of the Civil Rights Act of 1964. Title VII applies to employers with 15 or more employees, including state and local governments. It also applies to employment agencies and to labor organizations, as well as to the federal government."[66] The EEOC then defines sexual harassment:[67]

- The victim as well as the harasser may be a woman or a man. The victim does not have to be of the opposite sex.
- The harasser can be the victim's supervisor, an agent of the employer, a supervisor in another area, a co-worker, or a non-employee.
- The victim does not have to be the person harassed but could be anyone affected by the offensive conduct.
- Unlawful sexual harassment may occur without economic injury to or discharge of the victim.
- The harasser's conduct must be unwelcome.

Note: Although it is extremely important that this legislation exists—and that it protects anyone who is being harassed—sexual harassment law only applies to the workplace.

STREET HARASSMENT

The cultural attitude that women's bodies—as well as the bodies of women and men who challenge heterosexual norms—are public property shows up in our media and our political discussions. Much of the behavior related to that attitude takes place on the street, as we are going about our daily activities: walking to work, riding a bus, going for a jog. Not all victims of street harassment are women, but this form of intimidation is always connected to gender. The group Stop Street Harassment defines gender-based street harassment as "...unwanted comments, gestures, and actions forced on a stranger in a public place without their consent...directed at them because of their actual or perceived sex, gender, gender expression, or sexual orientation."[68]

Street harassment is a way of establishing masculine dominance—harassers make victims feel that they cannot go about their business without being approached by a potentially dangerous stranger who is sexually focused on them. Although many who engage in this behavior are hostile and expressing entitlement, not every street harasser is consciously trying to intimidate. Some may truly believe the attention is complimentary. Presenting street harassment as a compliment—something I've heard more than once on *Fox News*—reinforces traditional gender norms by assuming that all victims are heterosexual women who want and need the attention of male strangers. Presenting harassment as complimentary also ignores the sense of potential danger a victim experiences, which reinforces rape culture. While many people enjoy a sincere compliment in a safe environment, no one wants to feel threatened by unwanted attention—and no one enjoys being harassed.

Reproductive Justice

Motherhood or potential motherhood is a physical reality many women must navigate in one way or another because of our biology. Sex or rape plus a uterus can result in pregnancy, and menstruation (having a period) is a monthly reminder of this fact. We live potential—and sometimes actual—motherhood in our bodies from somewhere between the ages of 10 and 60, give or take a few years. Like sex itself, the way we view and treat its result is connected to sexism: we have a cultural attitude, evident in many laws and customs, that a woman shouldn't be able to set the terms around sex and her body, including pregnancy and motherhood.

The idea that women should be able to set these terms— relying on our consciences, our minds, and our bodies to guide us—about motherhood is known as **reproductive justice**. Reproductive justice has lasting consequences for a woman's ability to make an informed decision about the deep, abiding, and lifelong financial and emotional commitment of motherhood. Reproductive justice includes the following:

- ***Birth Control:*** Education about and access to contraception (or birth control) allows women to set the terms of when and with whom we will have sex, and whether or not we will become pregnant as a result.
- ***Fertility and Miscarriage:*** Education about fertility, infertility, and miscarriage, and support for those who are struggling with either infertility or miscarriage. Infertility is often a taboo subject, and women are made to feel that we have somehow fallen short of true womanhood if we wish to conceive and cannot. (Many men who struggle with infertility feel the same way about their masculinity.)
- ***Pregnancy:*** Education about pregnancy and the options surrounding it, including adoption and

abortion, with no pressure to make a particular choice. Access to quality healthcare for a pregnant woman. Protections in the workplace for pregnant women who must adjust their work duties for health reasons.

- *Abortion:* Access to legal abortion services, without harassment or unnecessary medical procedures.
- *Childcare:* Access to affordable childcare and support for working parents, such as maternity and paternity leave. Protections for children who are at risk of being targeted for violence due to the suspicions and fears of unconscious—and conscious—racism, homophobia, and other forms of discrimination.

A woman who cannot set the terms of her own reproductive life—when and whether she has children—is physically at the mercy of her body, and of motherhood, until menopause. There are several cultural assumptions about women, sex, and reproduction that keep patriarchy in place, including the following:

- Women shouldn't have sex if we don't want children.
- Limited or no access to reproductive health services such as contraception and abortion are an acceptable—and morally superior—substitute for a woman's informed choice.
- If a woman has children she must struggle to provide for them with little to no societal infrastructure (such as affordable daycare or family leave policies).

Policies connected to these attitudes about women and sex— combined with the attitudes about sexuality inherent in rape culture—ensure that many women are too preoccupied with motherhood to assert their own power, either internally or externally.

Does Sexism Affect Men?

I've discussed some of the ways that sexism hurts men—by requiring a limited view of masculinity based on hurting other people—in several topics. But most people who claim that sexism affects men (such as Men's Rights Advocates, discussed below) aren't talking about masculinity. They claim that men can be victims of "reverse sexism": treated as inferior and unequal to women, legally, culturally, and politically. So—is this possible? Can men be victims of sexism?

When we remember that sexism is about power, and that we live in a culture that gives more legal and cultural power to men— a patriarchy—it is clear that men are not the targets of sexism. The idea that women are inferior to men—not the reverse—is evident in everything from our media to our court cases, and I've given many examples of the power dynamics of sexism throughout this book. It is definitely a man's world, but that doesn't mean men don't have issues created by patriarchy. In other words, sexism affects men, just not in ways we usually discuss.

A patriarchy, with its reliance on traditional masculinity, portrays men in the following demeaning and harmful ways:

- *Breadwinners* who are here to make money for others—and they can never make enough.
- *Idiots* who don't know how to care for their children.
- *Robots* who have no emotions except anger, and who cannot discuss their own physical or emotional pain,

except to say they ignored or endured it as proof of manhood.

- *Violent predators* who can't control their sexual urges, and can't distinguish between consensual sex and rape.
- *Sexual machines* who don't feel or experience the emotions of sex, but can "go all night long" and want sex constantly, under all circumstances.
- *Lovers of warfare* who will take violence however they can get it—and who can't wait to prove their manhood on the battlefield, "giving up the body" for endless wars.

I'll discuss three of these stereotypes here—breadwinners, idiotic fathers, and robots.

Men as Breadwinners

Money is second only to muscles in defining manhood, and men know they should make plenty of it—enough to provide both security and luxury. This "breadwinner" concept is tightly tied to the concept of someone to win the bread for—a girlfriend to wow on a date and then woo with a fat diamond, a wife who is at home with kids while the breadwinner is out there making the money. This "ideal" of manhood never really fit millions of Americans—working-class families, many of them people of color, have always needed two incomes just to get by, and that breadwinner was always supposed to be coming home to a wife, not a husband. In other words, the breadwinner aspect of masculinity is tied to its other aspects, reinforcing the idea that a "real" man is both heterosexual and rich.

The breadwinner concept has done a great deal of harm to men and women of color. In *Ain't I a Woman*, bell hooks discusses the way our society has made black men feel less "masculine" and black women less "feminine" because of the necessity of two incomes in many black homes. Black women are often said to be "matriarchs," though, as a group, they don't hold political or financial power in our culture: "At the onset of the emergence of the matriarchy myth it was used to discredit black women and men. Black women were told that they had overstepped the bonds [*sic*] of femininity because they worked outside the home to provide economic support for their families and that by so doing they had de-masculinized black men. Black men were told that they were weak, effeminate, and castrated because 'their' women were laboring at menial jobs."[69]

The image of the "providing" man is deeply ingrained in the male psyche—it is part of our definition of manhood. And while it puts undue pressure on men to live up to an unrealistic ideal, it is firmly rooted in sexism: it keeps existing power structures in place by insisting that men are supposed to make more money than women. When you add racism and homophobia to the mix, you get a real brain game for men who don't fit the "ideal" in a variety of ways.

Men as Idiots: Dad the Dumbass

In 2012, Huggies diapers ran an ad campaign called "Have Dad Put Huggies to the Test" that depicted fathers as bumbling idiots, unable to figure out how to care for their children while mom is away. The campaign backfired as angry fathers, many of them stay-at-home dads, protested against the stereotype of dads who can't—or won't—care for their children well.[70] This is an old stereotype, left over from a fifties sitcom world—white middle-class women knew everything about the home and nothing about work, and white middle-class men could close a business deal but couldn't figure out how to close a diaper.

The sexism here is meant to keep mothers—whether they work outside the home or not—from expecting too much of the fathers of their children. And indeed mothers do more housework, and tend to drop out of the workforce more than fathers. But this arrangement is not because fathers don't want to be involved, or because they are incompetent when it comes to childcare—it is because our society isn't structured in a way that gives parents a lot of options. As Stephanie Coontz puts it in a *New York Times* article entitled "Why Gender Equality Stalled," "For more than two decades the demands and hours of work have been intensifying. Yet progress in adopting family-friendly work practices and social policies has proceeded at a glacial pace."[71]

Every family comes up with its own solutions to this problem: for most families, as Ms. Coontz describes, the bulk of childrearing and housekeeping falls to women, whether they work outside the home or not, and in spite of egalitarian attitudes from both parents. Despite an increase in stay-at-home fathers[72] and research showing the concerns of working fathers,[73] and despite a recent Pew study showing that both mothers and fathers are struggling with how to balance work and family,[74] the United States does not have policies that provide adequate maternity and paternity leave, flexible work conditions for working parents, and affordable, reliable daycare. These issues don't only affect mothers—they affect fathers too.

This approach to childcare policy leaves two-father families (and two-mother families, and single-parent families) out of the conversation and the equation. The idea that it's up to mothers to run the home because fathers are bad at it, while insulting to fathers, keeps existing power structures in place and makes equality in the workplace and at home difficult to achieve.

Men as Robots

As I've discussed in earlier topics, masculinity requires men to be tough—not to show their emotions, or even admit to having them. There are, of course, times when everyone needs to keep calm and carry on. And some people are less openly emotional than others. But to never admit to emotions like love, fear, depression, and anxiety because you think you shouldn't or can't isn't healthy—it requires men to pretend to be less than human. And the cost of that pretense can be very high.

As Rosalind Wiseman demonstrates in *Masterminds and Wingmen*, boys and young men are suffering: they have higher rates of learning disabilities than girls and much higher rates of suicide and imprisonment.[75] Hannah Rosin discusses similar concerns in *The End of Men*—she sees a society in which men are slowly slipping away. While Rosin attributes male struggles to the rise of female power—another version of a zero-sum game between men and women—Wiseman puts her finger on the button of a restrictive masculinity that doesn't allow boys and men to have feelings: "We don't acknowledge that boys wage sophisticated power plays and can be relentlessly targeted for humiliation, or that so many feel insecure about their bodies. We don't notice when some boys abuse power and then get allies to back them up while other boys seethe in silence."[76]

What begins in boyhood extends into manhood. Men do feel things beyond anger—they fall in love, they feel deep affection for their friends, they can be betrayed, they don't like to be mocked, they worry about aging and gaining weight, they can feel powerless at work—or useless without work—and they can be the victims of physical and emotional abuse. Add all of this to the constant pressure to prove manhood and the idea that men are supposed to be the hero in every situation, and you get a volatile mix of pain, with no acceptable ways to express it but violence or silence. Those who aren't violent—the majority of men—learn not to speak about their emotions and needs. To do so would be unmanly, and shameful.

The idea that men must be emotional robots is arguably the most important piece of the puzzle when it comes to patriarchy. As men struggle with the problems that traditional masculinity creates, along with the frustrations of life—like breakups and illnesses and job losses—they do so in an emotional vacuum. And that vacuum allows patriarchy to continue calling the shots for men as well as women—the masculinity that requires male silence in the face of male pain also requires male silence in the face of sexism in all its forms.

The Men's Rights Movement

There is no doubt that patriarchy causes men pain—we see it all around us. But because we approach gender issues as a zero-sum power game, we discuss men's issues as either completely separate from women's issues or as directly opposed to them. Too often, our national discussions about gender fail to recognize that many who work for female empowerment also work for male empowerment. Some people see that we don't discuss men's issues as often as women's and conclude that men are marginalized, and that it's time we began championing them instead of women. Enter the Men's Rights Movement.

The man who is credited as being the intellectual father of the Men's Rights Movement, Warren Farrell, sees all those depressing stats on boys that Rosalind Wiseman sees, and wants more organizations to address them. Farrell is quoted in a September 2014 article for *National Public Radio* (*NPR*): "'We need to know not only why are our sons committing suicide, but also why are our sons much more likely to be the ones to shoot up schools?' he says. 'We're all in jeopardy if we don't pay attention to the cries of pain and isolation and alienation that are happening among our sons.'"[77]

Farrell is right about our need to focus on boys, violence, and alienation, but he seems to be paying no attention to the work of Jackson Katz, Michael Kimmel, and others—quoted by Wiseman and nationally recognized as experts on masculinity. Those who don't follow masculinity studies—and therefore don't read about the connections between violence and masculinity and sexism and homophobia—could be drawn to the Men's Rights Movement as a possible solution to male issues. And that would be dangerous indeed, for the movement is rife with misogyny.

Men's Rights Advocates—or MRAs—use violently misogynistic language online. MRAs regularly harass women who are advocating for equal rights on social media. They are so obvious and undisguised in their hatred that the Southern Poverty Law Center has classified them as a hate group. The founder of the Men's Rights website, Paul Elam, claims to be seeking solutions for men that are other than those feminists seek: "[We can] seek solutions even if, God forbid, they're not solutions that are prescribed through the feminist lens."[78]

Ironically, the attacks on women that MRAs perpetuate—and their rhetoric of men's rights as something separate from and opposed to women's rights—serves to keep patriarchy in place, and therefore feed the very problems they seek to solve.

> **Note:** *Hatred of men is called **misandry**. Backlash (discussed below) has produced the common misconception that feminism*

promotes misandry. Feminism does not promote misandry; male and female feminists and their allies work to end sexism and intersecting forms of discrimination for the good of all.

Is Sexism Debatable?

I've covered a lot of examples, both from popular culture and politics, of the ways in which we debate sexism—from awards shows to political campaigns, from movies to motherhood, we discuss the specifics of how we should and do treat and portray women, and whether or not our treatment and portrayal of women is sexist. Listening to these debates, it's easy to conclude that sexism is something we can't fully define, because it's a matter of opinion rather than fact.

Recognizing Backlash

"Backlash" has become a buzzword, used within our media as a way to describe a response of any kind. There are backlashes to statements and actions from celebrities, politicians, and ordinary citizens. There are even backlashes to the backlashes. The term, as it is used in our media most of the time, simply means "a reaction."

When we are discussing sexism, backlash is indeed a reaction, and a negative one. In this context, backlash means our cultural reaction to attempts to change or abolish patriarchy. In her now-classic book *Backlash*, Susan Faludi emphasizes that backlash, like sexism itself, isn't always conscious: "The backlash is not a conspiracy, with a council dispatching agents from some central control room, nor are the people who serve its ends often aware of their role...."[79]

The United States has functioned as a patriarchy since its foundation. That means that when we attempt to change things— when we assert that sexism and other forms of discrimination are not an acceptable bedrock upon which to build either a vision of masculinity or systems of government, commerce, and thought—it makes people uncomfortable. The rules are changing, and we're defining the new rules as we go. Backlash comes along to try and re-establish the old order. Backlash takes many forms, including the ways we portray women in the media, the conversations we have about female roles in society (Faludi gives many examples of misinformation in our media that attempt to persuade women that we have to choose between work and family), and the solutions we present to our problems.

To recognize backlash, we must always keep the consequences of a statement, belief, or perspective in mind. For example, if a woman is arguing that "real men" need to assert their dominance and that is why young women aren't getting married, the result is a return to a stronger form of patriarchy. Similarly, if a discussion about sexism is presented as a debate in which both parties' opinions are equally informed—even if one of the people is an expert in the way patriarchy functions and the other is not—we don't really have to question or change sexist policies and practices. It's a matter of he says tomahto, she says tomato—an interesting conversation, but nothing to challenge the status quo.

GASLIGHTING

Sometimes in debates about sexism or other forms of discrimination—particularly online—people will use a tactic called **gaslighting** to make someone (often a woman) distrust her own experience, perceptions, and judgements. The term comes from the 1944 movie *Gaslight*, in which an abusive husband repeatedly dims and brightens the gaslights in their home while telling his wife he has no idea what's happening, causing her to question her sanity. In an argument or debate, a person using gaslighting will try to make his opponent think her perceptions are skewed or wrong. Gaslighting is not always conscious—it can be used unconsciously, as a defensive reaction. However, it can also be used consciously, as a manipulative tactic.

When watching or listening to a debate about sexism, pay close attention for gaslighting. Because we live in a patriarchy, all questions about sexism are discussed within a sexist environment in which sexism itself might be at play. Keep your eyes and ears open for statements designed to make a woman seem inferior within a debate: her reasoning isn't sound, she's being emotional (upset, hysterical, angry, shrill), she doesn't have the personal authority or ownership of the subject that her opponent does.

Again, these ideas might be used unconsciously in an argument, largely because sexism and self-esteem are so closely linked, for both women and men. Also, keep in mind that people who are learning about sexism and patriarchy—especially men— might feel they are being accused of conscious sexism or other forms of discriminatory thought. Context is everything: although gaslighting could be at play in all of them, a heated conversation with a friend is different from a Twitter debate with a misogynistic stranger, and both are different from a televised debate among pundits.

MANSPLAINING

The term **mansplaining**, unlike gaslighting, has entered mainstream conversation: it first appeared online shortly after Rebecca Solnit's piece in the *LA Times*, "Men Who Explain Things." Ms. Solnit didn't use the term in her article, but she gave a prime example of mansplaining, in which a man described her own book to her without acknowledging that she'd written it.[80]

Merriam-Webster describes mansplaining well: "...when a man talks condescendingly to someone (especially a woman) about something he has incomplete knowledge of, with the mistaken assumption that he knows more about it than the person he's talking to does."[81] Although women are usually on the receiving end of mansplaining, it isn't about us—it's not about female knowledge or behavior, about the way we perceive the world or the way we express our opinions and expertise, or even how and why we succeed. It's about traditional (or patriarchal) masculinity, which means it relies on sexist thoughts and beliefs.

A man who is attached to traditional definitions of manhood—including the idea that if he can't "best" a woman in a conversation or debate, he has failed to establish the necessary dominance of manhood—is going to feel that his masculinity is threatened when a woman knows more about a subject than he does. To deal with what he perceives as a threat, he pretends it doesn't exist—the woman is so woefully misinformed that she needs his guidance and expertise to understand the basics of the discussion, even if that discussion is about her career or field of knowledge.

In other words, mansplaining is a form of backlash, an attempt to maintain patriarchy. Like gaslighting, it can be used consciously or unconsciously, and must be understood within the context of a particular conversation.

Bringing It Back to Power

The test for whether or not something is sexist is, "Who or what purpose does this (joke, statement, question, practice, policy, belief, perspective) serve? What are its practical consequences, and for whom?" Any policy or practice or joke or statement or belief that reinforces the elements of patriarchy—including the idea that masculinity requires men to demean and hurt women and homosexual men—is sexist.

Modern patriarchy is not something that academics debate in an ivory tower while the rest of us are totally unaffected by it. Patriarchy is the basis of our society, even though that society no longer looks exactly like it did fifty years ago. Although our patriarchy has given way in many respects, it has remained stagnant or become stronger in others. When questions about sexism or other forms of discrimination arise, we must look to the structures of patriarchy and its concrete consequences. In other words, we must bring the conversation back to power and barriers to power—both internal and external.

Notes

1. Peggy McIntosh, "White Privilege and Male Privilege," University of Maryland Office of Diversity, http://www.odec.umd.edu/CD/GENDER/MCKIN.PDF. Originally published 1988.

2. Adrienne Rich, "Notes toward a Politics of Location," in *The Essential Feminist Reader*, ed. Estelle B. Freedman (New York: Modern Library, 2007), 372.

3. Bene't Holmes, "The White House Summit on Working Families Needs to Hear Worker Voices," A Voice for Working America, June 19, 2014, http://www.ufcw.org/2014/06/19/the-white-house-summit-on-working-families-needs-to-hear-worker-voices-a-guest-blog-by-our-walmart-member-benet-holmes/.

4. Emily Martin, "Illinois Commits to Protect Pregnant Workers," National Women's Law Center, August 26, 2014, http://nwlc.org/blog/illinois-commits-protect-pregnant-workers/.

5. Lilly Ledbetter, "About," accessed April 22, 2016, http://www.lillyledbetter.com/about.html.

6. Gail Collins, *When Everything Changed: The Amazing Journey of American Women from 1960 to the Present* (New York: Little, Brown and Company, 2009), 92.

7. Michael Kimmel, *Manhood in America: A Cultural History*, 3rd ed. (New York: Oxford University Press, 2012), 292.

8. Audre Lorde, "Learning from the 60s," in *Sister Outsider* (Berkeley: Crossing Press, 2007), 138.

9. Kimberlé Crenshaw, "Demarginalizing the Intersection of Race and Sex: A Black Feminist Critique of Antidiscrimination Doctrine, Feminist Theory, and Antiracist Politics," *University of Chicago Legal Forum* 1989 Issue 1, Article 8: 141-48,

http://chicagounbound.uchicago.edu/uclf/vol1989/iss1/8.

10. Ibid., 149.

11. Diane E. Levin, Ph.D., and Jean Kilbourne, Ed.d., *So Sexy So Soon: The New Sexualized Childhood and What Parents Can Do to Protect Their Kids* (New York: Ballantine Books, 2009), 5.

12. Peggy Orenstein, *Cinderella Ate My Daughter: Dispatches from the Front Lines of the New Girlie-Girl Culture* (New York: HarperCollins, 2011), 7-8.

13. Jackson Katz, "Tough Guise: Violence, Media, and the Crisis in Masculinity," Media Education Foundation (MEF) Channel, YouTube video, 7:02, uploaded October 4, 2006, http://www.youtube.com/watch?v=3exzMPT4nGI.

14. Rosalind Wiseman, *Masterminds and Wingmen: Helping Our Boys Cope with Schoolyard Power, Locker-Room Tests, Girlfriends, and the New Rules of Boy World* (New York: Harmony Books, 2013), 29.

15. Levin and Kilbourne, *So Sexy So Soon*, 33.

16. Naomi Wolf, *The Beauty Myth: How Images of Beauty Are Used Against Women* (New York: Harper Perennial, 2002), 280.

17. Ibid., 14.

18. Ibid., 157.

19. "Research on Males and Eating Disorders," The National Eating Disorders Association, accessed April 22, 2016 http://www.nationaleatingdisorders.org/statistics-males-and-eating-disorders.

20. Susan Bordo, *The Male Body: A New Look at Men in Public and in Private* (New York: Farrar, Straus, and Giroux, 1999), 71.

21. Ibid., 94-95.

22. Jackson Katz, *The Macho Paradox: Why Some Men Hurt Women and How All Men Can Help* (Naperville: Sourcebooks,

2006), 11.

23. Michael Kimmel, "Masculinity as Homophobia: Fear, Shame, and Silence in the Construction of Gender Identity," in *The Masculinities Reader*, ed. Stephen M. Whitehead and Frank J. Barrett (Cambridge: Polity, 2001), 279.

24. Ibid., 277.

25. Ibid., 272.

26. Gloria Steinem, *Revolution from Within: A Book of Self-Esteem* (New York: Little, Brown, and Company, 1993), 157.

27. American Psychological Association, Task Force on the Sexualization of Girls, *Report of the APA Task Force on the Sexualization of Girls*, (2007), http://www.apa.org/pi/women/programs/girls/report-full.pdf.

28. Christina Hoff Sommers, "No, Women Don't Make Less Money Than Men," *The Daily Beast*, February 1, 2014, http://www.thedailybeast.com/articles/2014/02/01/no-women-don-t-make-less-money-than-men.html.

29. Hanna Rosin, *The End of Men and the Rise of Women* (New York: Riverhead Books, 2012), 207.

30. George F. Will, "Michigan may offer the GOP's best answer to the so-called war on women," *The Washington Post*, April 11, 2014, http://www.washingtonpost.com/opinions/george-f-will-michigan-may-offer-the-gops-best-answer-to-the-so-called-war-on-women/2014/04/11/59817de0-c0d0-11e3-bcec-b71ee10e9bc3_story.html.

31. Rosin, *End of Men*, 29.

32. Ibid, 28.

33. Ibid., 30.

34. Ariel Levy, *Female Chauvinist Pigs: Women and the Rise of Raunch Culture* (New York: Free Press, 2005), 4.

35. Ibid., 112.

36. Suzanne Venker, "The war on men," *Fox News*, November 26 2012, http://www.foxnews.com/opinion/2012/11/24/war-on-men/.

37. Camille Paglia, "It's a Man's World, and It Always Will Be," *Time*, December 16, 2013, http://ideas.time.com/2013/12/16/its-a-mans-world-and-it-always-will-be/.

38. bell hooks, *Feminism is for Everybody: Passionate Politics* (Cambridge: South End Press, 2000), 61.

39. James Hibberd, "Sofia Vergara blasts critics of 'sexist' Emmy pedestal," Entertainment Weekly, August 26, 2014, http://insidetv.ew.com/2014/08/26/sofia-vergara-sexist-emmy-pedestal/.

40. Riane Eisler, *Sacred Pleasure: Sex, Myth, and the Politics of the Body—New Paths to Power and Love* (New York: HarperOne, 1995), 224.

41. Katz, *Macho Paradox*, 154.

42. "Rape and Sexual Assault," Bureau of Justice Statistics, accessed August 31, 2016, http://www.bjs.gov/index.cfm?ty=tdtp&tid=31.

43. "Sexual Assault," Rape, Abuse, and Incest National Network, accessed April 25, 2016, https://rainn.org/get-information/types-of-sexual-assault/sexual-assault.

44. "Defining Sexual Assault and Consent," Women's Center, Northwestern University, accessed April 25, 2016, http://www.northwestern.edu/womenscenter/issues-information/sexual-assault/defining-sexual-assault.html.

45. "Intimate Partner Violence: Definitions," The Centers for Disease Control and Prevention, June 19, 2016, http://www.cdc.gov/ViolencePrevention/intimatepartnerviolence/definitions.html.

46. MJ Breiding, KC Basile, SG Smith, MC Black, and RR Mahendra, *Intimate Partner Violence Surveillance: Uniform Definitions and Recommended Data Elements*, Version 2.0. (Atlanta: The Centers for Disease Control and Prevention, 2015), http://www.cdc.gov/violenceprevention/pdf/ipv/intimatepartnervio lence.pdf.

47. "Statistics," Rape, Abuse, and Incest National Network, accessed April 25, 2016, https://rainn.org/statistics.

48. Christopher P. Krebs, Ph.D. , Christine H. Lindquist, Ph.D. , Tara D. Warner, M.A. , Bonnie S. Fisher, Ph.D., Sandra L. Martin, Ph.D., *The Campus Sexual Assault Study*, December 2007, https://www.ncjrs.gov/pdffiles1/nij/grants/221153.pdf.

49. United States Department of Justice, *Crime in the United States*, 2010. (Washington, DC: Federal Bureau of Investigation, Uniform Crime Reports, 2011). Accessed via "Intimate Partner Violence: Consequences," Centers for Disease Control and Prevention, March 3 2015, http://www.cdc.gov/violenceprevention/intimatepartnerviolence/c onsequences.html.

50. Andrew R. Morral, Kristie L. Gore, Terry L. Schell, Barbara Bicksler, Coreen Farris, Bonnie Ghosh-Dastidar, Lisa H. Jaycox, Dean Kilpatrick, Stephan Kistler, Amy Street, Terri Tanielian and Kayla M. Williams, *Sexual Assault and Sexual Harassment in the U.S. Military: Highlights from the 2014 RAND Military Workplace Study*, (Santa Monica, CA: RAND Corporation, 2015), http://www.rand.org/pubs/research_briefs/RB9841.html.

51. M.J. Breiding, S.G. Smith, K.C. Basile, M.L. Walters, J. Chen, and M.T. Merrick, *Prevalence and Characteristics of Sexual Violence, Stalking, and Intimate Partner Violence Victimization— National Intimate Partner and Sexual Violence Survey* (United

States: Division of Violence Prevention, National Center for Injury Prevention and Control, CDC, 2011), http://www.cdc.gov/mmwr/preview/mmwrhtml/ss6308a1.htm.

52. National Congress of American Indians Policy Research Center, *Policy Insights Brief: Statistics on Violence Against Native Women* (NCIA Policy Research Center, 2013) http://www.ncai.org/attachments/PolicyPaper_tWAjznFslemhAffZ gNGzHUqIWMRPkCDjpFtxeKEUVKjubxfpGYK_Policy%20Insi ghts%20Brief_VAWA_020613.pdf.

53. Ibid.

54. Ibid.

55. Breiding, et. al., *Prevalence and Characteristics of Sexual Violence, Stalking, and Intimate Partner Violence Victimization.*

56. bell hooks, *Ain't I a Woman: black women and feminism* (Boston: South End Press, 1981), 52.

57. David Edwards, "Former Kentucky Prison Guard Avoids Jail for 25 Counts of Sexually Abusing Women Inmates," *Rawstory*, October 21 2014, http://www.rawstory.com/rs/2014/10/former-kentucky-prison-guard-avoids-jail-for-25-counts-of-sexually-abusing-women-inmates/.

58. Stephen A. Crockett Jr., "Officer Charged with Raping 8 Black Women Finds Support Online," *The Root*, September 2 2014, http://www.theroot.com/articles/culture/2014/09/officer_charged_with_raping_8_black_women_finds_support_online.html.

59. Sarah Larimer, "Disgraced ex-cop Daniel Holtzclaw sentenced to 263 years for on-duty rapes, sexual assaults," *The Washington Post*, January 22, 2016, https://www.washingtonpost.com/news/post-nation/wp/2016/01/21/disgraced-ex-officer-daniel-holtzclaw-to-be-sentenced-after-sex-crimes-conviction/.

60. Kirsten West Savali, "If Daniel Holtzclaw's Victims Were White, Everyone Would Know His Name," *The Root*, November 5, 2015, http://www.theroot.com/articles/news/2015/11/hate_crime_if_dani el_holtzclaw_s_victims_were_white_everyone_would_know.html.

61. Free Marissa Now, accessed May 6, 2016, http://www.freemarissanow.org/.

62. Victoria Law, "Against Carceral Feminism," *Truthout*, October 24 2014, http://www.truth-out.org/news/item/27028-against-carceral-feminism.

63. Charlotte Alter, "Todd Akin Still Doesn't Get What's Wrong With Saying 'Legitimate Rape,'" *Time*, July 17 2014, http://time.com/3001785/todd-akin-legitimate-rape-msnbc-child-of-rape/.

64. Sue Monk Kidd, *The Dance of the Dissident Daughter: A Woman's Journey from Christian Tradition to the Sacred Feminine* (New York: HarperCollins, 1996), 7.

65. Ibid., 8.

66. "Facts About Sexual Harassment," U.S. Equal Employment Opportunity Commission, accessed April 27, 2016, http://www.eeoc.gov/eeoc/publications/fs-sex.cfm.

67. Ibid.

68. "What is Street Harassment?" Stop Street Harassment, accessed April 27, 2016, http://www.stopstreetharassment.org/about/what-is-street-harassment/.

69. bell hooks, *Ain't I a Woman*, 75.

70. Janice D'Arcy, "Huggies revamps 'Dad Test' campaign after complaints," *The Washington Post*, March 12, 2012, https://www.washingtonpost.com/blogs/on-

parenting/post/huggies-revamps-dad-test-campaign-after-complaints/2012/03/12/gIQAHQng7R_blog.html.

71. Stephanie Coontz, "Why Gender Equality Stalled," *The New York Times*, February 16, 2013, http://www.nytimes.com/2013/02/17/opinion/sunday/why-gender-equality-stalled.html?pagewanted=all.

72. Jessica Dickler, "Stay-at-home dads: More men choosing kids over career," *CNN Money*, April 30, 2012, http://money.cnn.com/2012/04/30/pf/stay-at-home-dad/index.htm.

73. Brad Harrington, Fred Van Deusen, Jennifer Sabatini Fraone, Samantha Eddy, and Linda Haas, *The New Dad: Take Your Leave*, (Chestnut Hill, MA: Boston College Center for Work and Family, 2014), http://www.bc.edu/content/dam/files/centers/cwf/news/pdf/BCCWF%20The%20New%20Dad%202014%20FINAL.pdf.

74. Kim Parker and Wendy Wang, "Modern Parenthood: Roles of Moms and Dads Converge as They Balance Work and Family," Pew Research Center Social and Demographic Trends, March 14, 2013, http://www.pewsocialtrends.org/2013/03/14/modern-parenthood-roles-of-moms-and-dads-converge-as-they-balance-work-and-family/.

75. Rosalind Wiseman, *Masterminds and Wingmen*, 18.

76. Ibid., 21.

77. Joel Rose, npr, "For Men's Rights Groups, Feminism Has Come at the Expense of Men," September 2, 2014, http://www.npr.org/2014/09/02/343970601/men-s-rights-movement.

78. Ibid.

79. Susan Faludi, *Backlash: The Undeclared War Against American Women* (New York: Three Rivers Press, 1991), 13.

80. Rebecca Solnit, "Men who explain things," The Los Angeles Times, April 13, 2008, http://articles.latimes.com/2008/apr/13/opinion/op-solnit13.

81 "Mansplaining," Merriam-Webster Online, accessed April 27, 2016, http://www.merriam-webster.com/blog/mansplaining-definition-history.htm.

ABOUT THE SERIES

Thanks for reading *Defining Sexism*, the first in the series *Sexism in the U.S.: Questions and Answers*. If you enjoyed the book and found it helpful, I would appreciate a short review on Amazon and/or GoodReads. I am deeply grateful for your help in spreading the word.

The next book in the series, *Sexism and U.S. History*, will be available in the coming months. You can sign up to be notified of the next book as well as courses and special offers at https://elizabethhallmagill.com.

Made in the USA
San Bernardino, CA
31 March 2020